40 Common Errors
IN TENNIS
and How to Correct Them

Arthur Shay

Library of Congress Cataloging in Publication Data

Shay, Arthur.
    40 common errors in tennis and how to correct
them.

    Includes index.
    1. Tennis.   I. Title.
GV995.S45   1978   796.3′42   77-23708
ISBN 0-8092-7825-1
ISBN 0-8092-7824-3 pbk.

Published by Contemporary Books, Inc.
180 North Michigan Avenue, Chicago, Illinois 60601
Manufactured in the United States of America
Library of Congress Catalog Card Number: 77-23708
International Standard Book Number: 0-8092-7825-1 (cloth
                                    0-8092-7824-3 (paper)

Published simultaneously in Canada by
Beaverbooks
953 Dillingham Road
Pickering, Ontario L1W 1Z7
Canada

This book is for two of my favorite "tennists," Mike Hecht, a lapsed handball player who finally found cerebral calm in his new racquet, and author Herman Kogan, a net asset to journalism and tennis. It is also for the 30 million others of you who make the 40 common errors (and then some!) and strive to conquer them—because they are there.

Contents

Acknowledgments

I wish to thank Alan Schwartz, president of the Tennis Corporation of America and co-owner of the Mid-Town Tennis Club in Chicago, and his public relations counsel, Ivan Fuldauer, for the use of their 18 Mid-Town courts.

In awe of the accumulated tennis teaching knowledge of Mid-Town's staff, I would like, especially, to thank Mid-Town's chief instructor, the former tennis champion of Taiwan, Bob Huang.

It was Bob Huang who canvassed his staff for the 40 most common errors made by Mid-Town's 6,000 players and students. These are the staff members who modeled for the mistake and correction pictures that follow (having much more trouble doing the mistakes than the corrections!): Oscar Cisneros, Kevin Cummings, Bill Dutton, James Flesch, Tom Huff, Bill Kerr, Chuck Sheftel, Barbara Skurdall, Kim Southwell, Horace Watkis.

Introduction

The "tennist," one author's wonderful genderless word for *tennis player*, has been around for a little more than 100 years. The first and founding modern tennist, Major Walter Wingfield, a rich and fun-loving Englishman who sold sporting equipment, had of course seen "court tennis" played in its native France. Court tennis evolved as a castle courtyard pastime for monks and nobles even as other ball games evolved in Persia, South America, Africa, Asia (where heads of animals and human beings were used), and among the American Indians. The trick to court tennis (which is still played and was until recently dominated by an 80-year-old master named Pierre Etchebaster) was and is caroming the ball off brick walls, roofs, guardhouses, and other natural hazards of your average medieval courtyard. A sort of racquet and cloth-wrapped ball are used. The ball (most often made of ancient linen taken from the uniforms of dead soldiers) is fairly hard. The few standard court-tennis courts in France have standard obstructions these days.

Sports buff Wingfield had, of course, also seen Irish "fives" and English handball played in Britain. These games (the forerunners of American handball) were invented in prison, which may explain the widely held but inaccurate American notion that handball is a game of the lower middle class. After considerable experiment at his Nantclwyd estate, the Major produced an eight-page rule book, now priceless, for a game he called Sphairistike, or Lawn Tennis. Greek was commonly taught in the public schools of the day, so that few of the Major's guests had trouble translating "Sphairistike" into the equivalent of "Play Ball!"

The pamphlet and a short introductory course in the new game made the Major's well-attended Christmas tournament the success of the 1873 social scene, cold-weather clothes and all. Wingfield's hourglass-shaped court was bifurcated by an animal-catching net about three feet high.

Meanwhile, the All England Croquet Club at Wimbledon, a suburb of London, decided to increase its earning power by adding a few tennis courts. By 1877 the hourglass had given way to the rectangle and Wimbledon held its first tennis tournament. There were 22 entrants, and Spencer Gore won, paddling up the 26-yard-long, 9-yard-wide course as familiarly as he did on his shorter, enclosed racquets court. (Racquets is a squash-like, racquetball-like game played on a slate-walled court. There are fewer than two dozen such courts in the whole world today.)

So much for the incestuous history that contributed to the evolution of modern tennis as we try to improve on it. Except for one thing: For two years before the Wimbledon tournament, the father of United States tennis, Dr. James Dwight, was playing in and running a tournament on the second court in this country and laying the foundation for the United States Lawn Tennis Association, which has ridden herd on tennis ever since.

Why has tennis captured the hearts of some 28 million of us at this writing? Fun? Competition? Health? Healthful emotional outlet for aggressions? All of the above, say the doctors, the psychologists, the physiologists, the tennists. Plus one other wonderfully American characteristic—an inordinate need and desire to excel.

Until recently it was the Australians who excelled at tennis. Their minuscule population and California-type climate year after year produced the best players in the world. But now, thanks in part to the proliferation of the indoor tennis club, the improved level of instruction, and the desire to excel, the United States has begun to send incipient Jimmy Connorses, Tracy Austins, and Chris Everts out to match their Lavers and Newcombes.

The news that it is possible to earn half a million dollars a year has seeped down to our 13-year-olds and their parents—and this is, after all, a nation of determined parents and healthy, ambitious kids. The pot of gold at the end of the American rainbow has ever been a great motivating force. Mostly, though, tennis is fun, and most of us aspire to fun, not to world-class play. We'd just like to clobber our office friends, the guys from the neighborhood, the women who've given up bowling, the bigger kids on the block.

How can these laudable, patriotic goals be most easily achieved? Obviously, hard practice should produce results. But alas, practice alone and with good instruction isn't enough.

Which brings us to the tennis books. What a literature! In undertaking this book, I asked my wife, Florence, a rare-book dealer, to round up some "tennis books." In three days she located 75 of them. My favorite has a world-class player importuning beginning players he is supposed to be teaching to remain silent while watching a tournament so as not to bother the players' concentration!

To get in shape for doing my own book, I went through all the books I could buy, borrow, or find in the library—the weekend tennis books, the playing-better-players books, inside pro tips, digests of digests, tactical books, a sinister book for lefties (who should use a mirror on all right-hand instruction books), psych books, and so on. My verdict on all the books I saw was an irreverent shrug. Not one of them, I felt, properly demonstrated my non-tennist father Herman's approach to learning. "People learn by making mistakes," he taught me. "Then, when they know what they're doing wrong, they have to learn to correct it. Soon they do it right."

Mistakes; corrections. It sounds deceptively simple. Could I use the principle in a tennis book?

It was my good fortune at the time this was on my mind to do a *Time* magazine sports assignment at one of the country's largest tennis clubs, Mid-Town Tennis Club in Chicago. There, Chicago publicist Ivan Fuldauer introduced me to Mid-Town's chief pro, former Taiwan tennis champion Bob Huang (pronounced *Wong)*, a soft-spoken, hard-hitting player and teacher in his mid-thirties. It is Huang's daily task to supervise the teaching activities of some 20 men and women professionals. These pros teach some 100,000 people-hours of tennis a year to some 3,000 students of varying degrees of proficiency from rank beginner to collegiate champion.

"What is the one question students ask most?" I asked chief pro Huang, with my tape machine at the ready.

" 'What am *I* doing *wrong?*' " said Huang.

It was just a short step from there to evolving what we used to call on *Life* magazine a "shooting script."

Huang and his Mid-Town instructors met several times to contribute their candidates to our "wanted" list of "The 40 Most Common Errors in Tennis." Naturally, we weeded out duplicate entries in the mistake/correction sweepstakes, until each pro was assigned several errors to illustrate and correct. When our script was completed, we scheduled the classic *Life* or *Sports Illustrated* type of shooting session, a long day of photography. Amid the jeers of peers—as well as helpful hints as to assuming "correct" erroneous

attitudes on court so they would look just right—each pro stood, ran, served, received, flailed before my 250-exposure Nikon sequence camera.

After a thousand or so pictures, Bob Huang smiled. "I think we have it," he said, "with a few errors left over."

Having photographed most of the tennis greats of my time as a sports photographer—Laver, Connors, Evert, Newcombe, Smith, Briggs, Vilas, Borg, Casals, Ashe, Talbert, Trabert, Solomon, Gonzalez—and having read most of the books around, I must confess that my own tennis didn't move ahead until I saw what I was doing wrong. Then, for the first time in my life, I went out and clobbered Mike Hecht, a master tennis technician and a personal nemesis of mine. "It's a miracle," he said solemnly.

This is a simple book of modest ambition. It won't help you choose a racquet based on your Zodiac sign; it won't work on your psyche to make a winner out of you. All it aspires to do is *show you what you look like when you make a mistake—* and show you *what you should be doing instead.* As we go to press I am happy to report that the two dozen or so volunteer students who have just tried the mistake/correction system are so enthusiastic that Bob Huang has decided to use the book as a syllabus for some of Mid-Town's next class of 3,000 students at all levels.

Arthur Shay

Chapter 1
Grips and body position

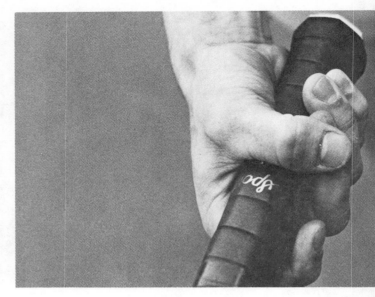

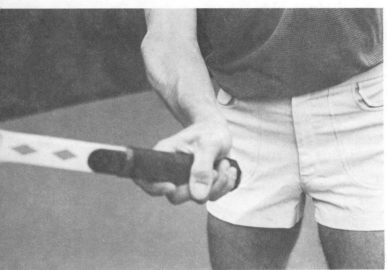

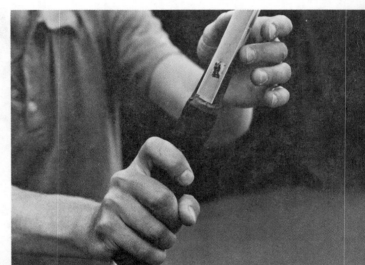

MISTAKE

Unorthodox forehand grip

An unorthodox forehand grip while stroking the ball immediately and after is responsible for cutting off most of the power that should flow from your body through your wrist into the ball. By gripping the racquet so as to make too great an angle between wrist and racquet you:

1. lose power
2. feel discomfort at the wrist
3. lose accuracy.

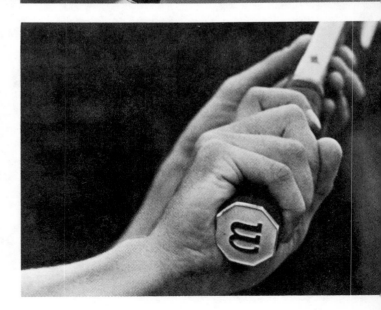

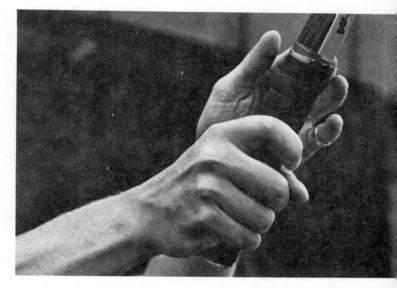

CORRECTION

A simple shake-hands grip should be used, with no severe angle between the wrist and the racquet. Form the classic "V" with thumb and forefinger on the shaft. Several practice swings should be done this way without the ball until you feel the smooth flow of power from your body through your shoulder, arm, and wrist. When you do this properly, you won't have to frantically cock that wrist and roll it over as you hit. Some players find that a tight squeeze at the moment of impact helps consolidate a good grip. Note the difference, too, in the follow-through pictures.

TIP: When you start to change from your unorthodox grip to this simpler one, try a few practice swings without the ball and *with your eyes closed.* For some reason, performing this short drill with eyes closed makes it easier to feel the transfer of power from body, through new wrist angle, to racquet.

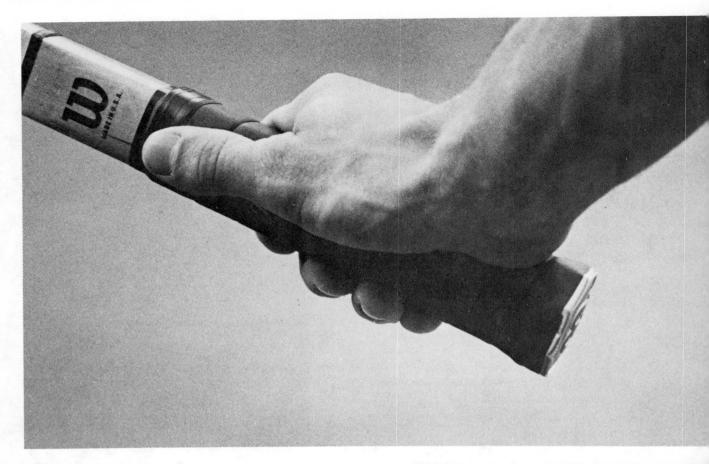

MISTAKE

Unorthodox backhand grip

Unorthodox backhand grips cause even more trouble than unorthodox forehand grips. That upraised thumb, that cocked wrist and errant finger will contribute to a loss of power that the average player tries to overcome with Herculean effort. The too-common grip shown causes a good percentage of "mechanical errors"— shots that go every which way.

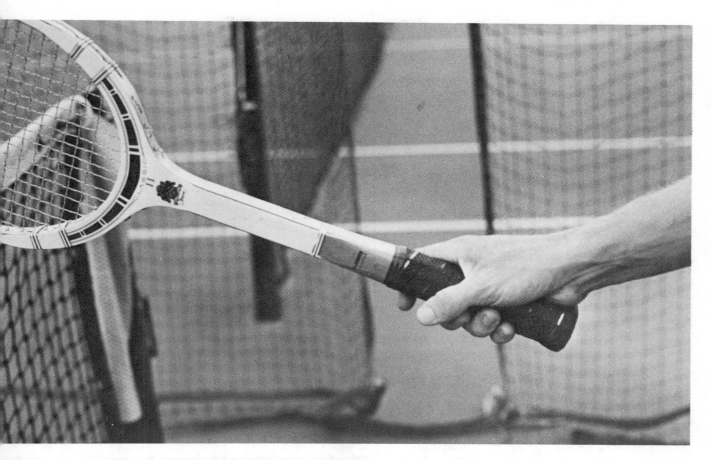

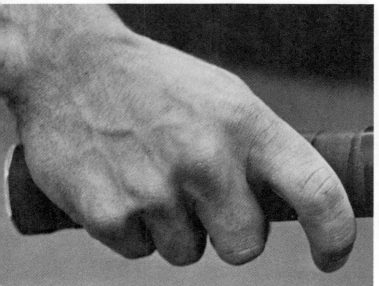

CORRECTION

The most effective backhand grip starts with the shake-hands forehand grip. As you run to make your backhand shot, flip the hand about a quarter-inch to the left—about an eighth of a turn. (It helps some players to think of turning the racquet toward the ground to keep their return low.) Another checkpoint is to align the index finger with the right bevel (hard angle) of the racquet. This lineup leaves no room for the trouble-making thumb to do anything but take its respective place with the other firmly wrapped fingers.

MISTAKE

Poor ready position

Tense, stiff, unready. These three strikes work against you from the moment your opponent serves. Your response to the serve will be late and not as well coordinated as it should be. You won't be able to race swiftly enough to the ball. If you assume a poor ready position, the chances are that you are not mentally set for the serve, either. Another strike against you!

CORRECTION

This is one of the easiest errors to correct. Keep your feet apart, about the width of your shoulders. Bend your knees slightly. Concentrate on your opponent's rhythm so that you can instantly adjust yours to it. The racquet is held in both hands out in front of the body. From the side, you resemble a good equestrian. Many good players develop a slight body and racquet sway that helps them keep from freezing in any one position while their opponent gets ready to serve. Concentration and good ready position are two of the things you can learn from watching tournament players in person or on TV.

MISTAKE

Improper transfer of the body weight and power from back foot to front foot during a stroke

The culprit in this common error is the straight front leg. If you keep that leg stiff and unbending, you are blunting the effect of one of the body's great springs—the knee. The side views of this error show the narrow power base resulting from a stiff leg. It affords a poor "platform" for hitting well. Thus, shots made from this narrow base are often erratic and of minimal power. Moreover, the player who tries to make a fast start can't do it well. Many of the players who so often seem to stumble over their own feet do so because of this easily correctable error.

CORRECTION

Practice bending and flexing your knees as you prepare to step into your shot. Bending your knees will keep you properly low and mobile. Often at a pro match you will see a player do three or four quick knee bends after a missed shot. This is a self-reminder to keep those knee springs loose and bouncy. They are the body's shock absorbers.

Stepping in to meet the ball broadens the power base set up by properly transferring the weight from back foot to front via the body. The crucial, coordinated, bouncy step-in should be thought of as the bridge across which the body's weight is transferred.

Ideally, all the body's movements come together a split second before impact with the ball. Tennis has this in common with the perfect swing in baseball or golf. As in those sports, a perfect shot in tennis is its own teacher; it feels right and transfers this feeling to you to help you recapture it again and again.

MISTAKE

Over-the-shoulder follow-through

In addition to poor transfer of weight and practically wrapping the racquet around the neck, this error is compounded by the failure to use the *non-racquet arm!* Poor power, improper balance, and lack of readiness for the next shot result from this error. Also, there will occasionally be a cracked head or shoulder—your own.

CORRECTION

The tightrope walker commonly keeps an umbrella in one hand and moves the free arm to retain balance. To correct a premature swing around the neck, a player should keep the free arm extended as the body assumes its sideways position for the shot. The non-racquet hand is a great secret weapon in perfecting body balance. Don't let it lock up or just hang there; let it swing freely and contribute to your coordination. High-speed movies and the computer have shown the free hand to be an important factor in properly aiming during fast play.

MISTAKE

Wrong foot leading into shots

When a player places the wrong foot frontward as she starts her stroke, she sets up a sorry chain of events. Even if she makes her shot, it is only an approximation of her potential shot, for it takes much extra effort to overcome that wrong foot lead. This error cuts power and placement accuracy, and is tiring relative to its correct cousin.

CORRECTION

Ideally, a player should arrive at her optimum hitting position a split second before her shot. The proper foot should be forward when the player arrives. Proper foot placement results in better control and the kind of stroke you can depend on and store in your growing arsenal. In some ways the backhand is a more natural stroke than the forehand, because you are swinging the way the racquet arm wants to go—away from the body. It is therefore wise to devote more of your practice time to getting the proper foot in the proper place for the backhand shot.

MISTAKE

Improper use of body weight after return to sideways position

In the scramble to return to good, coordinated positions during a series of shots, a player may lean back and spoil the whole maneuver by arriving at her position too soon and having to stroke the ball when her body isn't quite positioned to do it effortlessly and properly. This results in loss of power, overcompensation for this loss with uncoordinated arm movements, and general inaccuracy.

CORRECTION

The player must learn to time her arrival at the sideways position so that she can step in quickly, weight as usual going from back to front. This easy but important maneuver may be practiced by having the ball machine, if available, feed you waist-high fast balls. In play, learn to conserve your rushes to arrive neither too late nor too early. The object, as always, is the effortless swing; that is, the swing that appears to be effortless. If you sense that you are "looking good"—that is, coordinating—you will play better. Form and function are nowhere closer than in the art of tennis.

MISTAKE

Stroking while on one foot

Of course, great tennis shots have been accomplished on one foot. But we are not talking of desperation. The shifting of all the body's weight and power to one foot is generally a dangerous mistake, especially if it becomes a habit. Body imbalance results and shot control goes down to hit-or-miss proportions.

CORRECTION

A player should train the body's responses to assume the sideways stance, correct foot forward, weight transferring from back to front. The body's considerable power should be applied hardest to the ball a microsecond before contact with it.

MISTAKE

Premature opening of shoulders

The shoulders are part of a player's power arsenal. Most of the time on court, they should be facing one side of the court or the other. "Opening the shoulders"—that is, letting them face the net— too soon in the stroke will result in your using more arm than anything else in your shot, which wastes all the rest of your physical equipment. Weak returns and wild ones result from this common error.

CORRECTION

While concentrating on keeping the shoulders closed and facing the sidelines during the stroke, until the follow-through swings you around, you must also learn to let that non-racquet hand aid your balance. Your free arm can serve as a "seeing eye" that guides your shoulders into a proper response. Working through these details of the proper use of body weight and timing will eventually let you achieve optimum power no matter what your weight or physical condition. "Getting it all together" really works here.

MISTAKE

Leading racquet with elbow

This error is probably more to blame for cases of tennis elbow than anything else. Aside from putting unnecessary and unproductive stress on a perfectly good elbow, it will result in a push rather than a stroke. Examine the vast distance between the erring elbow and the body in this picture and make sure your elbow doesn't do the same in your backhand strokes.

CORRECTION

Keep your elbow tucked in—the closer to the body, the better. When you are in good swinging range, unleash your shot from the body, not the elbow. Let your body lead the elbow into your backhand. Conserve that elbow. You will need it.

MISTAKE

Hitting the ball too close to the body

This error, common even among good players, forces you to change your racquet stroke timing in order to make some kind of return. Generally, hitting the ball when it's too close to you will force you to shoot too quickly, without the moment of extra time and coordination necessary for a cross-court shot or other good offensive stroke. Generally, too, this stroke results in a hurried, unintentional slice that's often a setup for your opponent. This is because your racquet has arrived not for a stroke perpendicular to the floor, but at an angle.

22

CORRECTION

The shot should be stepped into and hit when it's ahead of the body, as most good tennis shots are. It is vital here to keep good arm and racquet distance at the moment of impact. Learning how to hit at the proper distance from your body will almost immediately elevate your play, for it will give you the time to hit fast or slow, flat or with a slice. It is a way of buying microseconds of time when you really need some—when you have proper distance from the ball.

Almost every tennis great who ever wrote on the subject, from Bill Tilden through today's authorities, agrees that "hitting the ball too close to the body" is the error common to most tennis players across the world. So, distance yourself. Run to the ball—but keep your distance.

MISTAKE

Interference by free hand

If you haven't learned to use your free hand as a balancing tool, try at least to keep it from becoming a hindrance. All kinds of serious problems—primarily, loss of freedom—will result when that free hand somehow gets in the way of your swing. If you have to reckon with it as an obstacle you're obviously doing something wrong.

CORRECTION

That free hand can become, as noted earlier, an important balancing aid for your body. You can feel this the moment you become aware of its possibilities. Then, you must practice both keeping it out of your way and making it work for you. Too often, the only time some players use that arm is to soften a fall.

MISTAKE

Not using the free hand

The free hand is most useful in the over-head shot. Unused, it is practically as harmful as it is when it obstructs a shot. Without the free arm working for you, you need extra effort to get the same forward thrust, and your flexibility will lag.

CORRECTION

Many good players find that they can most easily enlist the use of the free arm by using it as a spotter of identified flying objects, pointing out the ball for the well-coordinated right-hand smash.

Chapter 2
Strokes

MISTAKE

Chopping

It is sometimes a good stratagem to chop the ball, but not as a general rule. Too many players make the error of skying their racquets and bringing them down from the heavens to chop at the ball. This will often shorten the shot, dissipate power, and provide an easy winner for your opponent.

CORRECTION

Bring that racquet down, for starters. Start its arc to the ball from a lower position. Concentrate on making contact with a flat racquet. Work on a smooth follow-through by practicing the entire swing without the ball, then with it. The ideal shot should have your racquet finish up at shoulder height. Tennis is a game of arcs and curves, not chops and jerky movements.

MISTAKE

Backswing too short: forehand

Many players time their shots fairly well, arrive on time in good sideways position—and then blow the stroke, slicing the ball or barely nudging it over the net. Often the error is a simple one: not allowing enough of a backswing. They start the entire sequence of the shot without taking full advantage of a fully back-stretched racquet.

32

CORRECTION

Generally, the backswing should start with the racquet pointing to the back fence of your court, lined up with your body's sideways position. Now when you whip the racquet around to meet the ball, you will be able to "powder" it and also achieve a fine degree of accuracy unknown to the player with a backswing that is too short.

MISTAKE

Backswing too short: backhand

When the backswing is too short in a backhand stroke, you are pushing the ball instead of stroking it, or, at best, you are not getting all your potential power into the shot. Your weak returns will be catnip for good opponents. They will tend, also, to be less accurate than a shot made with a proper backswing that starts earlier.

CORRECTION

It helps some players to bring the racquet back for this shot using two hands, one as a balancing lever. Whether you can manage bringing the racquet way back with one hand or you use both hands, this is an important shot to practice. As in the forehand stroke, the racquet should be brought back until it points to the back fence before you start it forward to the ball. Accuracy is engendered during the longer arc of the racquet to the ball. Some players find that it helps to imagine two or three balls just behind the actual ball, so that their backswing enters the hitting zone in time to hit the ball properly.

MISTAKE

Excessive backswing

If you catch yourself doing this, the chances are you are hitting too many shots across the court and, no matter how strong you are, losing power.

CORRECTION

Swing the racquet back just far enough so that it is parallel to your body and points to the back fence or wall. If you recognize an excessive backswing as one of your faults, practice hitting the ball from an area six or eight feet from the back fence. This will help you judge when your racquet is indeed parallel with your body and pointing to the back fence. Your power and accuracy should develop in the area of the parallel backswing and should build all the way to the wrist and racquet.

MISTAKE

Vertical finish

After hitting a respectable backhand, many players loft the racquet skyward to finish the shot. Invariably this finish shortens the shot, and it accounts for many net-slappers. When too much top spin is imparted to the ball in this maneuver, the ball may hit the net or fall short of your aiming point. It often accounts for the unintended lob, too.

CORRECTION

The swing should carry through the ball (or those three imaginary balls if necessary). The follow-through should go straight out and *then* up. This adds power and control as well as depth. The correction of this error is vital to the "B" player en route to an "A" rating.

MISTAKE

Flicking the wrist

In the backhand stroke a player with otherwise good habits can develop the bad habit of flicking or snapping the wrist over too soon. This imparts excessive top spin to the ball and results in a serious loss of depth control. An opponent who spots this flaw in you can play you a step or two closer when you go for a backhand.

CORRECTION

During the backhand stroke the player should form an "L" between the wrist and the racquet at the moment of impact. The straight extension of the arm during the swing will prevent the wrist from flicking or snapping too quickly and short-circuiting the swing from its equal dependence on both wrist and arm.

MISTAKE

Lazy arm

There is a temptation on the part of some players to get through a game without moving too much. When a ball comes within arm's reach, they simply thrust the racquet out and try to spear the ball. Some spearers are quite adept. Others, of course, aren't. Prolonged spearing hurts the arm and produces weak, helter-skelter shots.

42

CORRECTION

Tennis is a game of pursuit and coordination. When the ball comes close, *move your body* to the best possible position from which you can launch a powerful return. The ideal is effortless strokes—not lazy flailing. Move it!

MISTAKE

Lazy legs

As in the common error of "Lazy Arm," "Lazy Legs" characterizes a player who would rather not move from a fixed position. When he (or she, of course) does move, there is minimal exertion and barely enough motion to get the ball—if indeed the player *does* make it to the ball. There are plenty of opportunities for stretching in tennis, but the casual one-legged stretch for the ball should not be one of them.

CORRECTION

Ideally, the player moves to the ball, assumes a proper stance, and sends the ball back as unreturnable as his ingenuity can manage. It is the legs that put you in this enviable position. Jog to get them in shape, do knee bends while warming up—but above all resolve that you will pursue that ball to the extent of your drive and stamina. Once there, you will be able to assume an effective offensive stance and fall back on your solidly learned ground strokes. You will be *playing* tennis, not playing *at* tennis. As your previously lazy legs put you in range, start concentrating on weight transfer. Soon you'll be playing better tennis.

MISTAKE

Leaning in

When a ball comes in short, many players have a tendency to bend forward, lean in, and make their shot from this uncoordinated position. The resulting "get," when it works, is barely a "get" but almost always a weak return that a good opponent will gobble up.

46

CORRECTION

When the ball comes in short, you must resist leaning, and then start taking long strides forward so that you can meet the ball with a smooth stroke, preferably from one side or the other in preference to a straight-ahead dump shot. You will thus be able to exert power and control instead of depending on luck and the confusion of your opponent.

Chapter 3
Service

MISTAKE

Improper service toss

It may be hard to believe, but a bad toss is accountable for about half of the serving errors committed! Cupping the ball too tight in the palm of the hand makes it difficult to release. It also makes it difficult to release the ball consistently on time and in good position. When the release is not done smoothly, precisely in the right place at the right time, the serve will inevitably suffer.

Most service-toss errors are compounded when players toss the ball too far to their left, throwing the server off balance and making necessary an immediate adjustment in striking the ball— even before you get into a rally!

CORRECTION

The ball should be cradled, as if it were an egg, in the fingers. The finger tips should delicately control the moment of release, height, and direction.

A good rule of thumb—of fingers, anyway—for right-handers is to toss the ball as high over the left toe as the racquet can reach and take it from there. If you feel as if you're falling over on the serve, experiment with your toss. It may be that simple.

MISTAKE

Bad service stance

If you plant your feet facing the net as you prepare to serve, you are immediately committing a grave fault—squandering much of your power. You will then have to make an effort to get some power into your serve. This unnecessary process will tire you too quickly and produce both inaccuracy and preordained bad weight transfer. When you're standing facing the net, both feet toeing the mark, you also risk falling if you swing hard enough.

CORRECTION

Face sideways. Toe the mark, or nearly toe it, with your left foot if you're right-handed. (That one left-handed tennist in six should either reverse all notations in books that refer to us non-sinisters, or watch himself in a mirror while practicing.) The transfer of power from back to front helps you achieve good serve potential. If necessary, your off hand can help balance your body as you serve.

MISTAKE

Lollipop serve

The lollipop or pitty-pat serve generally starts with a toss that's too low. Most of the potential power in the serve—and much of the accuracy—go down the tube, and the lollipop emerges to be gobbled up by your opponent.

CORRECTION

Work on the toss, on getting it precisely
to the height and distance that feels best
for you. In practicing, decide on this optimum height and distance; then don't set-
tle for less. Abort the serve if necessary
until you get the toss into the right spot
at the right moment. Your elbow must
stay up there to aid in the whip-of-the-
wrist that completes a good serve. But
get that toss down pat. It is one of the
simplest things to learn in all of tennis.

MISTAKE

Buried-head serve

Too many players get so wound up in their serves that their heads—more specifically, their eyes—end up studying their Adidas. Every time you take your eye off the ball in tennis, and almost all other ball sports, you risk the loss of directional control. In tennis, alas, this is especially true in the serve.

56

CORRECTION

You have now expunged the bad toss, replacing it with a neat little tailor-made toss just for your own service swing. OK—follow the rule of handball great Paul Haber: "I keep my eyes on the ball even during the time out." Don't lose sight of the ball from the moment it leaves your cushiony fingertips until it lands in your opponent's court and becomes an ace or is returned. In the latter case there is even more reason for keeping your eyes on the ball. Direction, control, tactics—all stem from this basic, simple procedure. If you keep your eyes on the ball it will be next to impossible to watch those shoes while you serve.

MISTAKE

Improper follow-through on service

The player fires a fairly good serve, but her follow-through comes down on her right side. Her uncoordinated serve may get a few serves over the net, but the wear and tear on her arm, which is being twisted in this error, make it unproductive and wearing. A habit like this often leads to shoulder pain—and sometimes a whacked right knee when the racquet strays from its terrible groove.

CORRECTION

Re-learn the serve if this is a veteran player's error. Good toss, good stance, and all that remains is to make a conscious effort to bring that follow-through down on the proper side of the body—in this case the left. Held as high as possible, the racquet should flow naturally to the left side for a good finish of an important shot.

MISTAKE

Racquet wraparound

Another common serving error, easily corrected when recognized, occurs on a serve: After the ball is hit, the racquet wraps around the server's free hand. This wraparound literally wraps the server up for long enough to lose a fast rally, certainly long enough to spoil a balanced approach to the next shot. Moreover, this error engenders terrible slices and chops. (A *slice* floats from right to left. A *chop* is a shot with lots of English, usually short.)

CORRECTION

If ordinary basic relearning of the serve proves too difficult, you can practice swinging the racquet as before—but pretend you're trying to brush your leading knee as you follow through. You may graze or crack your knee a few times, but you can turn this into a Zen type of advantage—and perhaps save a neck injury.

MISTAKE

Sunken elbow

The elbow is the culprit for those players unable to reach far up and out for a good overhand shot. For some reason many players tuck their hitting elbow close to the body and keep it down. This combination results in an unreliable return. Power, accuracy, and tactical edge all go out the window with this error.

CORRECTION

Practice reaching to the full extent of your arm and racquet. Swing without the ball as you warm up. (You're standing sideways, right?) Consolidate your circular motion and follow-through. Watch and feel for signs that your elbow is betraying you.

Chapter 4
Volleying

MISTAKE

Dropping the wrist

While volleying, the player either gradually or suddenly drops the wrist before the moment of contact between racquet and ball. This error causes an instant loss of power and control, reducing the stroke to a slice or near slice, a weaker return than intended. As with most poor shots, the player must then scamper for his next return, especially when playing a good opponent who can take advantage of the chain of events set up by the dropped wrist.

CORRECTION

Approaching the ball, the player must line his racquet up with the flight of the ball and hit it sharply ("punch" it) with wrist held firm to produce the best-coordinated impact possible. (If dropping the wrist is a long-overlooked habit, a firm squeeze of the racquet grip at the moment of contact is recommended as an instant reminder.) The thing to remember and to practice against opponent or machine is to keep the racquet facing in the direction of the shot. This is where control is born. Twenty minutes a day isn't too much practice time to devote to developing a well-controlled stroke that does not drop.

MISTAKE

Elbow up and out, racquet down

One of the most common errors in volleying occurs when the player gets carried away by the preparation motion for his ground stroke and continues it into backhand returns, so that as the racquet moves back, its head moves down. Usually, the elbow edges up and out at the same time. The combination weakens the crispness and punch of the return and often is the cause of late contact with the ball and the string of errors that lateness engenders.

CORRECTION

Some players use the free hand to guide the racquet into its proper elevated, diagonal position or help keep it there. (The free hand gently cradles the racquet at its throat.) Just before the ball is punched the free hand is removed. Traditionally, tennis players are somewhat awed by backhand problems, although most pros agree it is a more "natural" stroke than the forehand because it's less "involved" with the body. In this correction the main thing to practice is keeping the racquet head *up*, rather than back as in other ground strokes. The elbow *must* be "trained" not to get too far from the body.

MISTAKE

Late contact

During a volley, if you are intent on strategy, retrieving, and the other combat elements in competitive tennis, you might lapse into a simple error—late contact with the ball, or contact with it as it passes you. This often occurs when you are slightly overmatched and your opponent is hitting shots faster and farther than those you are accustomed to. Even if your late contacts are returned, they are generally of poor power and limited accuracy. A succession of these will make you feel as if you're being blasted off the court, when to a certain extent *you* are responsible.

70

CORRECTION

The proper point of contact between racquet and ball is out in front of the body, and a good third of all your motions in tennis should be devoted to getting your body into effective striking range of the ball. Tennis is also a forward-pressing game, and your practice should include much racing toward the ball—to meet it and hit it before it gets behind you, or hits you as you scamper to get a bead on it. Keeping the racquet up generally gives you another microsecond or so to hit the ball before that "hit" becomes a grievous "late contact."

MISTAKE

Scooping

Too often *lazy* players—not merely older players—keep both feet planted as the ball approaches them and fail to get their backs working for them. They then rely on the racquet as a scooping device and somehow retrieve and return the ball— usually without much force or control.

CORRECTION

You must learn to run to the ball and get the body into good sideways position for striking it. The racquet may have to be low, but the face of the racquet must still be parallel to the net, straight up and down. A good return in this manner will impart some underspin to the ball and make it tough to return.

MISTAKE

Body cross in backhand volley

In a backhand volley some players tend to swing the racquet at the ball and across their bodies. This generally results in but one kind of return—a cross-court return, usually wide and often out of bounds. A canny opponent will recognize this fault and have the advantage of knowing where to run for the ball each time he knows a backhand is coming.

74

CORRECTION

Sometimes the body-cross mistake is caused by overrunning the ball. This is of course corrected by slowing down and arriving in good time and with good form. The racquet should be kept up to correct this fault, and it should be pushed outward at the finish of the shot. This results in more depth as well as the crucial competitive edge gained by mastery of a variety of returns from a given situation.

MISTAKE

Upward push

The time for upward mobility is not the moment of contact with the ball in a forehand shot. Many players do everything right until that moment of truth—contact with the ball. At that moment they push the racquet upward to varying degrees. The result is that the ball is sent into the net or popped high over the net with minimum control.

CORRECTION

As in so many other tennis faults, footwork is preponderantly the villain in this error. Contributing, usually, is the racquet head's leaving the line of flight of the ball, usually to compensate for bad footwork. Both control and power come from moving the body into good position and then keeping the head of the racquet moving in the line of flight of the ball—not toward the ceiling or clouds.

MISTAKE

Pushing when near the net

In the quick reflexes demanded in net play some players tend to lose their cool when the ball comes toward the inside edge of their hitting shoulder. In a kind of gesture of self-defense the player pushes the racquet straight out to meet the ball. Result: ball in net; ball hits player; ball is in the lap of the Fates (not a bad lap if it's working for you . . . but . . .).

CORRECTION

Unless it's an absolute panic situation, the player should try to take a step backward and then step in with correct footwork to take the shot. Tennis is a sideways game for the most part, and you should "teach" this aphorism to your body. It will enhance your game and at any rate give you something to build upon for improvement.

MISTAKE

Facing the net

Facing the net for a stroke is almost always wrong in tennis, but especially so during an overhead shot. Here control and direction are quickly sacrificed to bad form.

CORRECTION

As soon as you see a lob coming at you, you should step back, right foot leading, and whirl around into a comfortable sideways position. As you do this you should draw the racquet up over your shoulder. When you have positioned your body properly behind the ball, swing the racquet up and out, through the ball, with smooth follow-through. This important shot is blown much too often in the excitement of the chase or of being near the ball while facing the net. Get sideways and win!

81

Chapter 5
Doubles

MISTAKE (Doubles)

Bad positioning

The server's partner (left) stays up too close to the net and too close to the alley. (The alley is the narrow lane between the inner singles boundary and the outer doubles line.) This error forces the server to cover more than a fair share of the court.

CORRECTION

Normal position of the server's partner should be six to eight feet from the net and halfway between the alley and the central service-line. He should face the person about to receive the serve from this position, which will give him the mobility required to cover his area.

MISTAKE

Serve receiver plays too far in

A good server will blast this opponent off the court, or, minimally, pin his ears back. Some "macho" players take this position as a dare. Macho is out these days.

CORRECTION

Wait for that serve well back in the court, usually near the baseline. It's easier to charge forward on a serve than backward. Practice receiving the serve. This is one of the most productive ways to use the ball machine. Learn to position yourself; don't try to "psych" an erratic or weak server.

MISTAKE

Receiver's partner too close to the net

Don't try to be a hero or heroine by coming in close on the serve to choke off returns. The odds are that many more will pass you than those you will retrieve. You will get only a small or inadequate piece of the ball on many unhappy returns, throwing your partner off and making things easy for your bloodthirsty opponents.

CORRECTION

Hang back until you're standing on the service-line or near it. Here the law of averages starts working *for* you. You'll also be much more fun and popular as a partner if you develop the good habit of keeping your distance intelligently.

MISTAKE

Bad team play

Playing partners who haven't given doubles much thought often work at cross-purposes. One such blighted area is the simple one of who follows the ball and who gets to make the shot. It is, most times, an error for one partner or the other to cover alone.

CORRECTION

Good doubles team members move back and forth with the ball, almost as if they were playing singles. Both hawk the ball. One of two important words may be shouted: "Mine!" or "Yours!" If this is missed the ball may slip through—like an infield hit in baseball. Generally, it will be easy for you to gauge a partner's strengths and weaknesses and match them with your own accordingly.

Good luck!

OFFICIAL RULES OF TENNIS

The Singles Game

Rule 1
Dimensions and equipment

The Court shall be a rectangle, 78 feet long and 27 feet wide. It shall be divided across the middle by a net, suspended from a cord or metal cable of a maximum diameter of one-third of an inch, the ends of which shall be attached to, or pass over, the tops of two posts, 3 feet 6 inches high, the center of which shall be 3 feet outside the Court on each side. The height of the net shall be 3 feet at the center, where it shall be held down taut by a strap not more than 2 inches wide. There shall be a band covering the cord or metal cable and the top of the net not less than 2 inches nor more than 2½ inches in depth on each side. The lines bounding the ends and sides of the Court shall, respectively, be called the Baselines and the Sidelines. On each side of the net, at a distance of 21 feet from it and parallel with it, shall be drawn the Service-lines. The space on each side of the net between the service-line and the sidelines shall be divided into two equal parts called the service-courts by the center service-line, which must be 2 inches in width, drawn halfway between, and parallel with, the sidelines. Each baseline shall be bisected by an imaginary continuation of the center service-line to a line 4 inches in length and 2 inches in width called the center mark drawn inside the Court, at right angles to and in contact with such baselines. All other lines shall not be less than 1 inch nor more than 2 inches in width, except the baseline, which may be 4 inches in width, and all measurements shall be made to the outside of the lines.

Rule 2
Permanent fixtures

The permanent fixtures of the Court shall include not only the net, posts, cord or metal cable, strap and band, but also, where there are such, the back and side stops, the stands, fixed or movable seats and chairs around the Court, and their occupants, all other fixtures around and above the Court, and the Umpire, Net-cord Judge, Foot-fault Judge, Linesmen and Ball Boys when in their respective places.

Rule 3
Ball—size, weight and bound
The ball shall have a uniform outer surface and shall be white or yellow in color. If there are any seams, they shall be stitchless. The ball shall be more than two and a half inches and less than two and five-eights inches in diameter, and more than two ounces and less than two and one-sixteenth ounces in weight. The ball shall have a bound of more than 53 inches and less than 58 inches when dropped 100 inches upon a concrete base. The ball shall have a forward deformation of more than .230 of an inch and less than .290 of an inch and a return deformation of more than .355 of an inch and less than .425 of an inch at 18-pound load. The two deformation figures shall be the averages of three individual readings along three axes of the ball and no two individual readings shall differ by more than .030 of an inch in each case. All tests for bound, size and deformation shall be made in accordance with the Regulations.

Rule 4
Server and receiver
The Players shall stand on opposite sides of the net; the player who first delivers the ball shall be called the Server, and the other the Receiver.

Rule 5
Choice of sides and service
The choice of sides and the right to be Server or Receiver in the first game shall be decided by toss. The player winning the toss may choose, or require his opponent to choose:

(a) The right to be Server or Receiver, in which case the other player shall choose the side; or

(b) The side, in which case the other player shall choose the right to be Server or Receiver.

Rule 6
Delivery of service
The service shall be delivered in the following manner. Immediately before commencing to serve, the Server shall stand with both feet at rest behind (i.e., farther from the net than) the baseline, and within the imaginary continuations of the center-mark and sideline. The Server shall then project the ball by hand into the air in any direction and before it hits the ground strike it with his racquet, and the delivery shall be deemed to have been completed at the moment of the impact of the racquet and the ball. A player with the use of only one arm may utilize his racquet for the projection.

Rule 7
Foot fault
The Server shall throughout the delivery of the service:

(a) Not change his position by walking or running.

(b) Not touch, with either foot, any area other than that behind the baseline within the imaginary extension of the center-mark and sideline.

Rule 8
From alternate courts
(a) In delivering the service, the Server shall stand alternately behind the right and left Courts, beginning from the right in every game. If service from a wrong half of the Court occurs and is undetected, all play resulting from such wrong service or services shall stand, but the inaccuracy of the station shall be corrected immediately it is discovered.

(b) The ball served shall pass over the net and hit the ground within the Service Court which is diagonally opposite, or upon any line bounding such Court, before the Receiver returns it.

Rule 9
Faults
The Service is a fault:

(a) If the Server commits any breach of Rules 6, 7 or 8;

(b) If he miss the ball in attempting to strike it;

(c) If the ball served touches a permanent fixture (other than the net, strap or band) before it hits the ground.

Rule 10
Service after a fault
After a fault (if it be the first fault) the Server shall serve again from behind the same half of the Court from which he served that fault, unless the service was from the wrong half, when, in accordance with Rule 8, the Server shall be entitled to one service only from behind the other half. A fault may not be claimed after the next service has been delivered.

Rule 11
Receiver must be ready
The Server shall not serve until the Receiver is ready. If the latter attempts to return the service, he shall be deemed ready. If, however, the Receiver signifies that he is not ready, he may not claim a fault because the ball does not hit the ground within the limits fixed for the service.

Rule 12
A let
In all cases where a let has to be called under the rules, or to provide for an interruption to play, it shall have the following interpretations:

(a) When called solely in respect of a service, that one service only shall be replayed.

(b) When called under any other circumstances, the point shall be replayed.

Rule 13
The service is a let
The service is a let:

(a) If the ball served touches the net, strap or band, and is otherwise good, or, after touching the net, strap or band, touches the Receiver or anything which he wears or carries before hitting the ground.

(b) If a service or a fault be delivered when the Receiver is not ready (see Rule 11).

Rule 14
When receiver becomes server
At the end of the first game the Receiver shall become the Server, and the Server Receiver; and so on alternately in all the subsequent games of a match. If a player serves out of turn, the player who ought to have served shall serve as soon as the mistake is discovered, but all points scored before such discovery shall be reckoned. If a game shall have been completed before such discovery, the order of service remains as altered. A fault served before such discovery shall not be reckoned.

Rule 15
Ball in play till point decided
A ball is in play from the moment at which it is delivered in service. Unless a fault or a let be called, it remains in play until the point is decided.

Rule 16
Server wins point
The Server wins the point:

(a) If the ball served, not being a let under Rule 13, touches the Receiver or anything which he wears or carries, before it hits the ground;

(b) If the Receiver otherwise loses the point as provided by Rule 18.

Rule 17
Receiver wins point
The Receiver wins the point:

(a) If the Server serves two consecutive faults;

(b) If the Server otherwise loses the point provided by Rule 18.

Rule 18
Player loses point
A player loses the point if:

(a) He fails, before the ball in play has hit the ground twice consecutively, to return it directly over the net (except as provided in Rule 22 (a) or (c); or

(b) He returns the ball in play so that it hits the ground, a permanent fixture, or other object, outside any other lines which bound his opponent's Court (except as provided in Rule 22 (a) and (c); or

(c) He volleys the ball and fails to make a good return even when standing outside the Court; or

(d) He touches or strikes the ball in play with his racquet more than once in making a stroke; or

(e) He or his racquet (in his hand or otherwise) or anything he wears or carries touches the net, posts, cord or metal cable, strap or band, or the ground within his opponent's Court at any time while the ball is in play; or

(f) He volleys the ball before it has passed the net; or

(g) The ball in play touches him or anything that he wears or carries, except his racquet in his hand or hands; or

(h) He throws his racquet at and hits the ball.

Rule 19
Player hinders opponent
If a player commits any act either deliberate or involuntary which, in the opinion of the Umpire, hinders his opponent in making a stroke, the Umpire shall in the first case award the point to the opponent, and in the second case order the point to be replayed.

Rule 20
Ball falling on line—good
A ball falling on a line is regarded as falling in the Court bounded by that line.

Rule 21
Ball touching permanent fixture
If a ball in play touches a permanent fixture (other than the net, posts, cord or metal cable, strap or band) after it has hit the ground, the player who struck it wins the point; if before it hits the ground, his opponent wins the point.

Rule 22
Good return
It is a good return:

(a) If the ball touches the net, posts, cord or metal cable, strap or band, provided that it passes over any of them and hits the ground within the Court; or

(b) If the ball, served or returned, hits the ground within the proper Court and rebounds or is blown back over the net, and the player whose turn it is to strike reaches over the net and plays the ball, provided that neither he nor any part of his clothes or racquet touch the net, posts, cord or metal cable, strap or band or the ground within his opponent's Court, and that the stroke be otherwise good; or

(c) If the ball be returned outside the post, either above or below the level of the top of the net, even though it touches the post, provided that it hits the ground within the proper Court; or

(d) If a player's racquet passes over the net after he has returned the ball, provided the ball pass the net before being played and be properly returned; or

(e) If a player succeeds in returning the ball, served or in play, which strikes a ball lying in the Court.

Rule 23
Interference
In case a player is hindered in making a stroke by anything not within his control except a permanent fixture of the Court,

or except as provided for in Rule 19, the point shall be replayed.

Rule 24
The game
If a player wins his first point, the score is called 15 for that player; on winning his second point, the score is called 30 for that player; on winning his third point, the score is called 40 for that player, and the fourth point won by a player is scored game for that player except as below:

If both players have won three points, the score is called deuce; and the next point won by a player is called advantage for that player. If the same player wins the next point, he wins the game; if the other player wins the next point the score is again called deuce; and so on until a player wins the two points immediately following the score at deuce, when the game is scored for that player.

Rule 25
The set
A player (or players) who first wins six games wins a set; except that he must win by a margin of two games over his opponent and where necessary a set shall be extended until this margin be achieved.

Rule 26
When players change sides
The players shall change sides at the end of the first, third and every subsequent alternate game of each set, and at the end of each set unless the total number of games in such set be even, in which case the change is not made until the end of the first game of the next set.

Rule 27
Maximum number of sets
The maximum number of sets in a match shall be 5, or, where women take part, 3.

Rule 28
Rules apply to both sexes
Except where otherwise stated, every reference in these Rules to the masculine includes the feminine gender.

Rule 29
Decisions of umpire and referee
In matches where an Umpire is appointed, his decision shall be final; but where a Referee is appointed, an appeal shall lie to him from the decision of an Umpire on a question of law, and in all such cases the decision of the referee shall be final, except that in Davis Cup matches the decision of a linesman can be changed by the Referee, or by the Umpire with the consent of the Referee.

The Referee, in his discretion, may at any time postpone a match on account of darkness or the condition of the ground or the weather. In any case of postponement the previous score and previous occupancy of Courts shall hold good, unless the Referee and the players unanimously agree otherwise.

Rule 30
Play shall be continuous from the first service till the match be concluded; provided that after the third set or when women take part, the second set, either player is entitled to a rest, which shall not exceed 10 minutes, or in countries situated between Latitude 15 degrees North and Latitude 15 degrees South, 45 minutes, and provided further that when necessitated by circumstances not within the control of the players, the Umpire may suspend play for such a period as he may consider necessary. If play be suspended and be not resumed until a later day, the rest may be taken only after the third set (or when women take part the second set) of play on such later day, completion of an unfinished set being counted as one set. These provisions shall be strictly construed, and play shall never be suspended, delayed or interfered with for the purpose of enabling a player to recover his strength or his wind, or to receive instruction or advice. The Umpire shall be the sole judge of such suspension, delay or interference, and after giving due warning he may disqualify the offender.

(a) Any nation is at liberty to modify the first provision of Rule 30, or omit it from its regulations governing tournaments, matches, or competitions held in its own country, other than the International Lawn Tennis Championships (Davis Cup and Federation Cup).

(b) When changing sides, a maximum of one minute shall elapse from the cessation of the previous game to the time players are ready to begin the next game.

The Doubles Game
Rule 31
The above rules shall apply to the Doubles Game except as below.

Rule 32
Dimensions of court
For the Doubles Game, the Court shall be 36 feet in width, i. e., 4½ feet wider on each side than the Court for the Singles Game, and those portions of the singles sidelines which lie between the two service-lines shall be called the service sidelines. In other respects, the Court shall be similar to that described in Rule 1, but the portions of the singles sidelines between the baseline and service-line on each side of the net may be omitted if desired.

Rule 33
Order of service
The order of serving shall be decided at the beginning of each set as follows:

The pair who have to serve in the first game of each set shall decide which partner shall do so and the opposing pair shall decide similarly for the second game. The partner of the player who served in the first game shall serve in the third; the partner of the player who served in the second game shall serve in the fourth, and so on in the same order in all the subsequent games of a set.

Rule 34
Order of receiving
The order of receiving the service shall be decided at the beginning of each set as follows:

The pair who have to receive the service in the first game shall decide which partner shall receive the first service, and that partner shall continue to receive the first service in every odd game throughout that set. The opposing pair shall likewise decide which partner shall receive the first service in the second game and that partner shall continue to receive the first service in every even game throughout that set. Partners shall receive the service alternately throughout each game.

Rule 35
Service out of turn
If a partner serve out of his turn, the partner who ought to have served shall serve as soon as the mistake is discovered, but all points scored, and any faults served before such discovery shall be reckoned. If a game shall have been completed before such discovery, the order of service remains as altered.

Rule 36
Error in order of receiving
If during a game the order of receiving the service is changed by the receivers it shall remain as altered until the end of the game in which the mistake is discovered, but the partners shall resume their original order of receiving in the next game of that set in which they are receivers of the service.

Rule 37
Ball touching server's partner is fault
The service is a fault as provided for by Rule 9, or if the ball served touches the Server's partner or anything he wears or carries; but if it touches the Receiver or anything which he wears or carries, not being a let under Rule 13(a), before it hits the ground, the Server wins the point.

Rule 38
Ball struck alternately
The ball shall be struck alternately by one or the other player of the opposing pairs, and if a player touches the ball in play with his racquet in contravention of this Rule, his opponents win the point.

(Rules reprinted by permission of the United States Lawn Tennis Association)

Index